READ & RESPOND

Bringing the best books to life in the classroom

Activities based on Tom's Midnight Garden
By Philippa Pearce

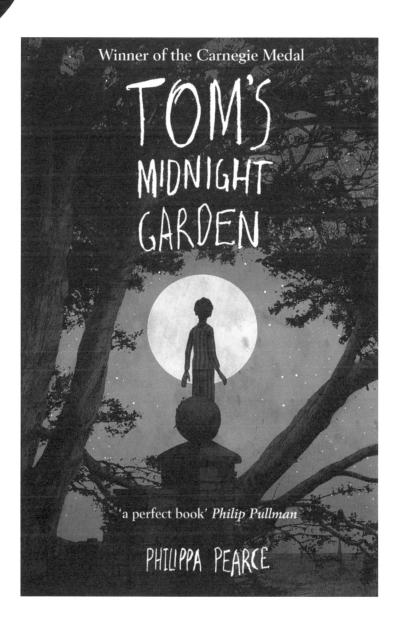

Winner of the Carnegie Medal

TOM'S MIDNIGHT GARDEN

'a perfect book' *Philip Pullman*

PHILIPPA PEARCE

FOR AGES 7–11

Scholastic Education, an imprint of Scholastic Ltd
Book End, Range Road, Witney, Oxfordshire, OX29 0YD
Registered office: Westfield Road, Southam, Warwickshire CV47 0RA

Printed and bound by Ashford Colour Press
© 2018 Scholastic Ltd
1 2 3 4 5 6 7 8 9 8 9 0 1 2 3 4 5 6 7

British Library Cataloguing-in-Publication Data
A catalogue record for this book is available from the British Library.
ISBN 978-1407-17507-2

Extracts from *The National Curriculum in England, English Programme of Study* © Crown Copyright. Reproduced under the terms of the Open Government Licence (OGL). http://www.nationalarchives.gov.uk/doc/open-government-licence/version/3

Due to the nature of the web, we cannot guarantee the content or links of any site mentioned. We strongly recommend that teachers check websites before using them in the classroom.

Authors Sally Burt and Debbie Ridgard
Editorial team Audrey Stokes, Vicki Yates, Marion Archer, Suzanne Adams
Series designer Neil Salt and Alice Duggan
Designer Alice Duggan
Illustrator Dave Smith/Beehive Illustration

Acknowledgements
The publishers gratefully acknowledge permission to reproduce the following copyright material:
Oxford University Press for the use of the extract text from *Tom's Midnight Garden* by Philippa Pearce (Oxford University Press, 2015). Copyright © Philippa Pearce, 1958.

Photographs
Page 8: Philippa Pearce © Helen Craig, by permission of the Philippa Pearce Estate

Every effort has been made to trace copyright holders for the works reproduced in this book, and the publishers apologise for any inadvertent omissions.

How to use Read & Respond in your classroom...

Read & Respond provides teaching ideas related to a specific well-loved children's book. Each Read & Respond book is divided into the following sections:

ABOUT THE BOOK AND AUTHOR

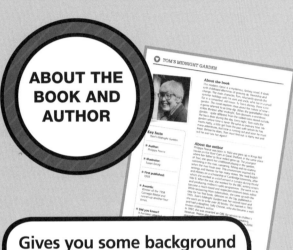

Gives you some background information about the book and the author.

GUIDED READING

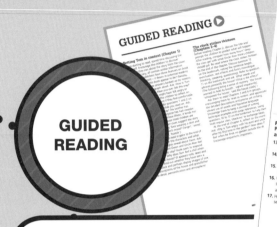

Breaks the book down into sections and gives notes for using it with guided reading groups. A bookmark has been provided on page 12 containing comprehension questions. The children can be directed to refer to these as they read.

SHARED READING

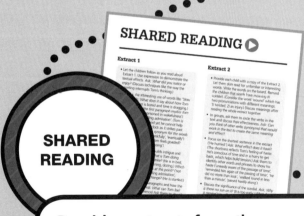

Provides extracts from the children's book with associated notes for focused work. There is also one non-fiction extract that relates to the children's book.

GRAMMAR, PUNCTUATION & SPELLING

Provides word-level work related to the children's book so you can teach grammar, punctuation and spelling in context.

PLOT, CHARACTER & SETTING

Contains activity ideas focused on the plot, characters and the setting of the story.

GET WRITING

Provides writing activities related to the children's book. These activities may be based directly on the children's book or be broadly based on the themes and concepts of the story.

TALK ABOUT IT

Has speaking and listening activities related to the children's book. These activities may be based directly on the children's book or be broadly based on the themes and concepts of the story.

ASSESSMENT

Contains short activities that will help you assess whether the children have understood concepts and curriculum objectives. They are designed to be informal activities to feed into your planning.

❝The titles are great fun to use and cover exactly the range of books that children most want to read. It makes it easy to explore texts fully and ensure the children want to keep on reading more.❞

Chris Flanagan, Year 5 Teacher, St Thomas of Canterbury Primary School

Activities

The activities follow the same format:

- **Objective:** the objective for the lesson. It will be based upon a curriculum objective, but will often be more specific to the focus being covered.

- **What you need:** a list of resources you need to teach the lesson, including printable pages.

- **What to do:** the activity notes.

- **Differentiation:** this is provided where specific and useful differentiation advice can be given to support and/or extend the learning in the activity. Differentiation by providing additional adult support has not been included as this will be at a teacher's discretion based upon specific children's needs and ability, as well as the availability of support.

The activities are numbered for reference within each section and should move through the text sequentially – so you can use the lesson while you are reading the book. Once you have read the book, most of the activities can be used in any order you wish.

CURRICULUM LINKS

Section	Activity	Curriculum objectives
Guided reading		Comprehension: To develop positive attitudes to reading and understanding of what they read.
Shared reading	1	Comprehension: To draw inferences such as inferring character's feelings, thoughts and motives from their actions.
	2	Comprehension: To discuss their understanding and explain the meaning of words in context.
	3	Comprehension: To discuss and evaluate how authors use language, including figurative language, considering the impact on the reader.
	4	Comprehension: To distinguish between…fact and opinion. To summarise the main ideas… and identify key details.
Grammar, punctuation & spelling	1	Vocabulary, grammar and punctuation: To use…dashes to indicate parenthesis.
	2	Transcription: To spell words containing the letter string 'ough'.
	3	Vocabulary, grammar and punctuation: To use semicolons, colons…to mark boundaries between independent clauses.
	4	Vocabulary, grammar and punctuation: To use colons and semicolons in lists.
	5	Transcription: To distinguish between homophones and other words which are often confused.
	6	Vocabulary, grammar and punctuation: To use modal verbs…to indicate degrees of possibility.
Plot, character & setting	1	Composition: To consider how authors have developed characters.
	2	Comprehension: To make comparisons within and across books.
	3	Comprehension: To summarise the main ideas drawn from more than one paragraph.
	4	Comprehension: To identify and discuss themes and conventions in and across…writing.
	5	Composition: To consider how authors have developed characters.
	6	Comprehension: To ask questions to improve their understanding.
	7	Comprehension: To identify how language, structure and presentation contribute to meaning.
	8	Comprehension: To identify how language, structure and presentation contribute to meaning.

Section	Activity	Curriculum objectives
Talk about it	1	Spoken language: To consider…different viewpoints.
	2	Spoken language: To gain, maintain and monitor the interest of the listener(s).
	3	Spoken language: To participate in discussions…and debates.
	4	Spoken language: To participate in…role play.
	5	Spoken language: To use relevant strategies to build their vocabulary.
	6	Spoken language: To participate in…presentations.
Get writing	1	Vocabulary, grammar and punctuation: To recognise vocabulary and structures that are appropriate for formal speech.
	2	Composition: To use…organisational and presentational devices to structure text.
	3	Composition: To describe settings, characters and atmosphere and integrate dialogue.
	4	Composition: To use…organisational and presentational devices to structure text.
	5	Composition: To ensure the consistent…use of tense throughout a piece of writing.
	6	Composition: To evaluate and edit by assessing the effectiveness of their own and others' writing.
Assessment	1	Spoken language: To listen and respond appropriately.
	2	Comprehension: To understand what they read by asking and answering questions.
	3	Comprehension: To discuss and evaluate how authors use…figurative language, considering the impact on the reader.
	4	Composition: To read aloud…with appropriate intonation to make the meaning clear.
	5	Vocabulary, grammar and punctuation: To recognise the difference between structures typical of informal speech and…formal speech.
	6	Spoken language: To give well-structured descriptions…for different purposes, including for expressing feelings.

Key facts
Tom's Midnight Garden

◉ **Author:**
Philippa Pearce

◉ **Illustrator:**
Susan Einzig

◉ **First published:**
1958

◉ **Awards:**
Winner of the 1958
Carnegie Medal and
runner-up another four
times.

◉ **Did you know?**
It has been adapted into
a film, a stage play, and
three television versions.

About the book

This modern classic is a mysterious, fantasy novel. It deals with childhood dilemmas of growing up, friendship and change. The main character, Tom, reluctantly spends the summer holidays with his aunt and uncle, who live in a small flat in a converted, old house. To Tom's dismay, there is no garden. The novel explores ideas about the nature of time – a genre referred to as time-slip. When the grandfather clock strikes thirteen after midnight, Tom discovers a wondrous garden – quite different from the rubbish bins stored outside the back door during the day. Every night, Tom visits the garden where time is never the same as ordinary time. He meets Hatty, a little girl from the past with whom he has many adventures, but time is running out and soon he must leave. Before he does, Tom must find out: is Hatty real and will he ever see her again?

About the author

Philippa Pearce was born in 1920 and grew up in Kings Mill House on the River Cam in Great Shelford, in the same place where her father (a flour miller) grew up. The youngest of four, she spent her childhood playing in the garden, swimming in the river, canoeing, fishing and ice-skating when the river froze over. This environment inspired the settings and themes for her many stories. She read English and History on a scholarship at Cambridge University, after which she worked as a civil servant in London during World War II. After the war, she worked for the BBC writing scripts and producing children's radio programmes. She went on to become a much-loved and respected children's book editor. While recovering from tuberculosis, she came up with the idea for her first book, *Minnow on the Say*, published in 1955. *Tom's Midnight Garden* was her second novel and she went on to write over 30 books. She married in 1963 and had a daughter, Sally Christie, who also became a well-known children's author.

In 1997, she was awarded an OBE for services to children's literature. Pearce also enjoyed lecturing, public speaking, storytelling and writing short stories until her death in 2006.

About the illustrator

Susan Einzig was an illustrator, fine artist and art teacher. She was born in 1922 in Berlin, Germany, but left for England before the outbreak of World War II where she attended the Central School of Art and Design – her brother and mother followed but her father died in a concentration camp. During the war, she worked as a technical draughtsman for the War Office. After the war, she worked as an illustrator and art tutor, and later became a senior lecturer at Chelsea School of Art and Design. She died in 2009.

GUIDED READING ▶

Setting Tom in context (Chapter 1)

Before starting to read, spend time discussing the book itself. Encourage the children to discover everything they can about the story from the cover. While covers vary, all contain similar information. Ask: *Why do publishers have these features on book covers?* (selling point – it draws in potential readers) *What genre does this book appear to be?* (fantasy, adventure) Encourage answers backed up by reasons.

Read the first paragraph aloud. Ask: *How is Tom feeling?* (angry, upset) *Have you ever felt this way?* Share a time when you might have felt angry or frustrated to encourage the children to reflect on their experiences and share if they feel comfortable. Ask the children to consider questions 1 and 2 on the bookmark (page 12) while you read on. Ask: *Why is Tom being sent away?* (his brother has measles) Survey whether anyone has had measles. Explain that measles is a serious illness, it tends not to be seen nowadays because most children are vaccinated. Ask: *What other clues suggest the story is set in the past?* (late 50s: Tom wearing a shirt and tie) *What words reveal Tom's mood?* ('anger', 'weep', 'raged', 'bitterly', 'angrily', 'hostile'.)

Encourage the class to read in pairs to the end of the chapter, focusing on the characters and what their actions and thoughts reveal about them. Ask: *How do you think Aunt Gwen and Uncle Alan feel about Tom coming to stay?* Invite pairs to respond with reasons. Ask: *Why does Tom feel a chill when he first enters the house?* (It appears cold, dead and unwelcoming.) Find out whether they have seen a grandfather clock and perhaps display images of one. Highlight descriptions of the house and grandfather clock (the detail, personification and atmosphere).

The clock strikes thirteen (Chapters 2–4)

Before reading Chapter 2, discuss the title and prompt the children to predict what will happen. After reading, compare how many hours' sleep the class get with what Uncle Alan thinks children should get. Re-read where the clock strikes thirteen to the end of the chapter. Discuss question 12 on the bookmark, noting the sentence length, punctuation, text effects and Tom's monologue (thinking, speaking, questioning). Refer to question 11 on the bookmark and ask: *What words and phrases personify the house? What is the effect?* (The following bring a sense of mystery: 'the house seemed to hold its breath', 'sighed impatiently', 'whispered the house', 'said the house coldly'.)

Ask them to read Chapters 3 and 4 in groups, encouraging them to 'read as writers' and appreciate the detailed descriptions and precise yet striking, vibrant use of words and figurative language. Encourage them to keep a journal of writing technique examples with page references, using questions 10 to 12 on the bookmark to help them. Hold regular class 'check-ins' to exchange ideas.

At the end of Chapter 4, reflect on the events. Ask: *Why is Tom angry with his aunt and uncle after his first time in the garden? How does Tom feel when he finds no garden outside the door?* Encourage empathetic responses.

The garden comes alive (Chapters 5–11)

Read Chapter 5 to the class, encouraging the children to visualise the garden. Extend their vocabulary by collecting unfamiliar features and names to build a class bank of new or interesting words. Ask: *Why is Tom 'uneasily aware of the passage of time'?* (He is concerned how long he's been away.) *What does Tom discover at the end of the chapter?* (Time in the garden is different to ordinary time.) *Why is he relieved?* (He hasn't broken his promise to his uncle.) *What does this suggest about his character?* (He is honourable, his word is important.)

Ask groups to read to the end of Chapter 9, focusing on questions 3 and 14 on the bookmark, and choosing passages to read aloud to each other. Invite volunteers to summarise events in each chapter. Ask: *What shows time is passing in the garden?* (different seasons, times of day and weather) *Is time chronological in the garden? What clue tells you this?* (No, the fir tree reappears.)

Read to the end of Chapter 11. Ask: *How do Tom and Hatty get to know each other?* (play and talk) *How are they similar?* (age; both lonely and love the garden) *What does 'fear lifted from Hatty like a cloud' mean? What type of figurative speech is this? What additional evidence suggests her fear?* (she was no longer afraid; simile; she is concerned about getting into trouble for wet or dirty clothes)

Discuss question 13 on the bookmark and demonstrate examples, such as the end of Chapter 7 where third-person narrative shifts into 'omniscient' third person. Ask: *What's the difference between third-person and omniscient third-person narrators?* (Both narrate events from outside; omniscient third-person narrators are all-knowing – they know what everyone thinks and feels, and what will happen – often characterised by talking to the reader, and interpreting or foreshadowing events.)

Time passing (Chapters 12–16)

The geese incident in Chapter 12 is a turning point. Read to the end of Chapter 16 and review the chapters together. Ask: *What evidence suggests Tom's view of Hatty has changed?* (he no longer contradicts her; her words make him 'feel warm and kind') Discuss question 8 on the bookmark, focusing on what the aunt says and the younger Hatty. List techniques the author uses to provide background information and clues as you read. At the start of Chapter 13, ask: *What is the effect of personifying Time?* (It adds a sense of urgency, that time may be running out.) Ask the children to discuss question 16 on the bookmark. Ask: *Who do you think is right?* This is an important element of the mystery so elicit thoughtful, creative responses based on textual evidence.

Focus on the atmosphere shift in the garden. Ask: *What events suggest all is not well?* (Abel's anger; realisation that Abel can see Tom and thinks Tom comes from Hell; Hatty falling) Invite words to describe Tom's mood at the end of Chapter 16.

In search of Hatty (Chapters 17–23)

Read Chapters 17 and 18 with you as narrator and volunteers as various characters. Encourage children to consider question 17 on the bookmark and identify clues to show time is passing. (For example, the grey in Hatty's aunt's hair, James having grown into a man, Hatty looking older and telling him months go by between visits.) Ask: *Why is James concerned about Hatty?* (She's not growing up emotionally as much as physically; she has no money or prospects.) *How old do you think Hatty is now?* Encourage them to look for suggestions backed by evidence.

Ask the children to read Chapters 19 to 23 in groups and then discuss question 7 on the bookmark. Ask: *How do Tom's and Uncle Alan's ideas of proof differ?* (Uncle Alan is more scientific/ factual; Tom is more imaginative.) *Why does Tom make Hatty promise to keep her skates in her secret place?* (To prove his theories about time – see themes below.)

Encourage the children to reflect on what the season turning to winter symbolises. (Their time in the garden is coming to an end.) Ask: *How does Tom believe he's solved his problem of time?* (Hours after midnight are not part of ordinary time – they are endless.)

Time comes full circle (Chapter 24–end)

Briefly discuss question 6 on the bookmark, referring to the turning point in Chapter 12. Invite predictions on the climax before reading Chapters 24 and 25 together. At the end of Chapter 25, discuss question 17 on the bookmark. Ask: *How did Tom get the skates he was holding when Uncle Alan found him?* Invite a volunteer to explain how Peter could have appeared in the garden and Tom in Peter's dream and build a class understanding of the climax and how the author creates drama.

Survey what endings the children enjoy and invite suggestions as to how this story ends, before reading the final two chapters. Refer to questions 4 and 9 on the bookmark and invite opinions and reflections on whether they enjoyed this ending.

Structure

Together discuss question 5 on the bookmark, using the time shifts as a springboard for discussions on story structure. Ask: *How are the time shifts different from flashbacks?* (Tom enters past time rather than earlier events in the same narrative being recounted out of order.) Invite opinions on whether there is a separate 'problem, build-up, climax and resolution structure' in Hatty's time and in ordinary time.

Challenge them with questions relating to the problem of time by asking: *When does the story begin? Is Tom a time-traveller? Does Tom's 'present' really overlap with Hatty's 'present'? Or is it only in his dreams?* Encourage the children to compile questions of their own along these lines.

Style

The novel was written in 1958 which means some vocabulary may be old-fashioned or unfamiliar even in Tom's 'present'. Encourage use of dictionaries to look up unfamiliar words and discuss the role of word selection in giving the story such visual and emotional depth. This is what makes the novel a rich modelling resource for evocative and descriptive writing. Ask: *How would the story be different if it was written as a first-person narrative?* Experiment with children recasting parts from Tom's or Hatty's perspective as narrator.

Setting

Tom arrives in his summer holidays but it's spring when he first enters the garden. Ask: *How do the seasons reflect what happens in the story?* (Accept thoughtful answers and reference to the text.) *Is the setting for the book real or imaginary?* (The garden was once real but Tom's ability to enter it makes it fantasy – especially as his ability to enter it is linked to Mrs Bartholomew's dreams – yet her dreams are of real events.)

Characters

Tom and Hatty are the main characters, with Tom as the protagonist. Ask: *Who is the antagonist in the story?* (Hatty's aunt is the antagonist in her time, but, unintentionally, Tom's uncle and aunt could also be considered antagonists: they don't understand, they're not part of Tom's midnight life and represent the threat of being sent home and away from the garden.) Discuss whether the house and time can be considered characters, since both are personified at different times. Ask: *In what ways was time both Tom's friend and his enemy?* (Refer to the end of Chapter 19.)

Themes

Time is the most pervasive theme. The problem and mystery of time for Tom lies at the core of the book's plot, with its importance highlighted by personification and capitalisation. Other themes, however, thread through, such as loneliness and friendship. Various PSHE issues can also be addressed with reference to the storyline such as: bullying; sibling relationships; kindness and unkindness; being orphaned; the gulf between the rich, imaginative world of childhood and the prosaic realities of the adult world.

Tom's Midnight Garden
by Philippa Pearce

Focus on... Meaning

1. Describe Tom's character when we first meet him.

2. What was Tom's reaction to being sent to his aunt and uncle? Why did he feel that way?

3. How do Tom and Hatty change throughout the book? Give examples.

4. What clues hinted at Mrs Bartholomew's identity throughout the book?

Focus on... Organisation

5. Is the book written in chronological order?

6. What is the turning point in the book? What is the climax?

7. How does 'time' underpin the story as a theme?

8. What devices does the author use to allow Tom (and the readers) to learn about Hatty's past?

9. What is satisfying about the book's ending?

Tom's Midnight Garden
by Philippa Pearce

Focus on... Language and features

10. Find examples of vocabulary that show the story was written and set a long time ago.

11. Identify examples of similes, metaphors and personification. How do they add to the story?

12. What techniques does the author use to build mystery and tension?

Focus on... Purpose, viewpoints and effects

13. Who narrates the book? How is this effective?

14. How does each character in the garden feel about Hatty?

15. Explain how time is different for Hatty and Tom.

16. What makes both Tom and Hatty sure they are real, but each other are ghosts?

17. Hatty gradually finds it harder to see Tom. What does this imply?

SHARED READING ▶

Extract 1

- Let the children follow as you read aloud Extract 1. Use expression to demonstrate the textual effects. Ask: *What did you notice or enjoy?* (Discuss techniques like the way the counting interrupts Tom's thinking.)

- Consider the interesting use of words like 'Slow silence'. Ask: *What does it say about how Tom is feeling?* (Tom is bored and time is dragging.) *What phrase in the first paragraph implies Tom feels trapped?* ('imprisoned in wakefulness') *Explain Tom's 'unwilling admiration'.* (Tom is in a cross, irritable mood yet he cannot help being intrigued by the clock as it strikes past the correct hour.) *Give a synonym for the words 'And at last'.* ('finally', 'thankfully', 'eventually') *Which words imply that Tom feels goaded?* ('proclaimed', 'jeered', 'pressing')

- Consider how the author builds intrigue and tension in the text. Ask: *What is Tom doing when the clock begins to strike?* (He is in bed, lying awake, counting, yawning, dozing.) *Which words show Tom's feelings at this point?* ('not amused', 'irritation', 'unwilling admiration', 'sleepily') *How does this change?* (He is startled.)

- Consider the final two paragraphs and how the atmosphere changes. Ask: *What can Tom feel 'in his bones'?* (a difference) Ask them to identify words and phrases that indicate a change in atmosphere.

- Read the final sentence together and ask a volunteer to identify the personification. Ask: *What tells us that Tom is feeling drawn into something?* (The house seems to be daring him to do something.)

Extract 2

- Provide each child with a copy of the Extract 2. Let them skim read for unfamiliar or interesting words. Write the words on the board. Remind the children that words have meaning in context. (Consider the word 'wound' which has two pronunciations with different meanings: 1) twisted; 2) an injury.) Discuss meanings after reading the whole extract together.

- In groups, ask them to circle the verbs in the text and discuss their effectiveness. Ask: *Can you think of other verbs (synonyms) that would work in the text to create the same meaning and effect?*

- Focus on the shortest sentence in the extract ('He hurried.') Ask: *What effect does it have?* (The shortness reflects Tom's feeling of haste. He's conscious of time and in a hurry to get back, which helps build tension.) Ask them to identify other words and phrases to show his haste ('uneasily aware of the passage of time', 'reminded him again of the passing of time', 'he did no more than look', 'walked round in less than a minute', 'passed hastily along').

- Discuss the significance of the sundial. Ask: *Why is there no sun on it?* (It is too early.) *What does it remind him of?* (the time, and the urgency of getting back to bed)

- The author describes the garden in detail. Ask: *How would you summarise the garden in just a couple of words?* (for example, 'idyllic', 'beautiful', 'flourishing', 'a paradise', 'happy', 'haven')

- Focus on the figurative language bringing the tree and sundial to life. Discuss its effectiveness and how it differs from factual writing.

Extract 3

- Read Extract 3 with the children following. Consider the setting. Ask them to compare this setting to the first part of the story. Ask: *What has changed?* (It is winter, Tom and Hatty are not together in the garden and they're skating, not playing.)

- Consider the characters. Ask: *How does the author show how their relationship has matured?* (Hatty is older than Tom; she feels safe with him; they are happy together, skating in silence, alone, in sync.)

- Discuss meaning. Ask: *What are passers-by meant to infer from the signboard outside the ale house?* (It's an invitation for skaters and others to stop, stay, relax and buy a drink!) *What's a hoax?* (a joke or trick) *What does the author compare Hatty's and Tom's arms and legs to?* (clock pendulums)

- Ask them to identify clues hinting at Tom's invisibility. (The men couldn't see Tom; only Hatty has a shadow.) Ask: *Why doesn't this seem to bother Hatty?* Encourage discussion.

- Discuss similes, metaphors and personification and how they add to the story. Ask them to highlight the personification: the alehouse, Hatty's shadow, the willow trees, the ice and Ely's tower. ('a lonely river-side alehouse'; 'Hatty's black shadow flitted along'; 'Only the willows along the bank watched them; and the ice hissed with their passage'; 'Ely's tower plays a game with the traveller')

- Discuss the historical context and the reference to unaccompanied girls. Ask: *Why were the skaters 'mostly men'?* (It was considered unacceptable for girls to be out alone. Girls were considered the 'weaker sex'.)

Extract 4

- Hand out copies of Extract 4. Read only the heading and ask the children to predict whether the extract is fiction or non-fiction. (It is non-fiction.) Ask: *How does the layout suggest a factual text?* (Headings and paragraphs with key sentences highlighted.) Now ask them to skim the extract to get the general idea before reading the enlarged extract paragraph-by-paragraph.

- Paragraph one: Ask: *What is another name for measles?* (Rubeola) *How is it spread?* (airborne, through coughing or sneezing where people are in close contact) *What is a deadly disease?* (a disease that can kill you) *What do the words 'successful' and 'effective' refer to in this context?* (The vaccine was able to prevent measles.)

- Paragraph two: Encourage them to describe measles' symptoms to a partner. They should try to remember as many facts as possible. Ask: *Can measles be cured?* (no) *How can it be treated?* (rest, drink liquids and stay in quarantine)

- Paragraph three: Ask: *How many children have died from measles?* (millions) *Is this a fact or an opinion?* (It is a fact, although the number is not specific.) *Why did this happen?* (no vaccines, combined with poor hygiene and lack of quarantine – young children share germs easily through proximity in play)

- Paragraph four: Ask: *Why was measles almost forgotten?* (the vaccination was/is so effective) *What has caused recent outbreaks of measles?* (More people are choosing not to vaccinate.)

- Ask them to summarise the key information in four sentences – one per paragraph. Invite them to share their summary with a partner.

Extract 1

The Clock Strikes Thirteen

Slow silence, and then the grandfather clock struck for twelve. By midnight his uncle and aunt were always in bed, and asleep too, usually. Only Tom lay still open-eyed and sullen, imprisoned in wakefulness. And at last—One! The clock struck the present hour; but, as if to show its independence of mind, went on striking—Two! For once Tom was not amused by its striking the wrong hour: Three! Four! 'It's one o'clock,' Tom whispered angrily over the edge of the bedclothes. 'Why don't you strike one o'clock, then, as the clocks would do at home?' Instead: Five! Six! Even in his irritation, Tom could not stop counting; it had become a habit with him at night. Seven! Eight! After all, the clock was the only thing that would speak to him at all in these hours of darkness. Nine! Ten! 'You are going it,' thought Tom, but yawning in the midst of his unwilling admiration. Yes, and it hadn't finished yet: Eleven! Twelve!

'Fancy striking midnight twice in one night!' jeered Tom, sleepily. Thirteen! Proclaimed the clock, and then stopped striking.

Thirteen? Tom's mind gave a jerk: had it really struck thirteen? Even mad old clocks never struck that. He must have imagined it. Had he not been falling asleep, or already sleeping? But no, awake or dozing, he had counted up to thirteen. He was sure of it.

He was uneasy in the knowledge that this happening made some difference to him: he could feel that in his bones. The stillness had become an expectant one; the house seemed to hold its breath; the darkness pressed up to him, pressing him with a question: Come on, Tom, the clock has struck thirteen—what are you going to do about it?

Extract 2

The Footprints in the Dew

Tom, made uneasily aware of the passage of time, crept back by the way he had come—back into the garden. He began to make himself familiar with it—its paths and alleys and archways, its bushes and trees. He noted some of its landmarks. At a corner of the lawn, a fir-tree towered up above all the other trees of the garden; it was wound about with ivy, through which its boughs stuck out like a child's arms through the wrappings of a shawl. On the high south wall, half covered by the sporting of a vine, there was a sundial; it was surmounted by a stone sun with stone rays, and its chin was buried in curly stone clouds— looking like his father's chin covered with shaving lather, Tom thought. To one side of the sundial, under a honeysuckle archway, was a door: Tom might have tried it, but the sight of the sundial, even without the sun upon it yet, had reminded him again of the passing of time. He hurried.

At the greenhouse, he did no more than look through the glass at the plants inside, and at the water tank, where a gleam came and went—perhaps a goldfish waking. The raised cucumber-frames by the greenhouse were walked round in less than a minute. He passed hastily along beside the aviary, where fan-tail pigeons were beginning to pick their way across the brick floor.

He criss-crossed the kitchen-garden beyond the asparagus beds: fruit trees and strawberry beds and bean poles and a chicken-wire enclosure where raspberry canes and gooseberry bushes and currant bushes lived sheltered from the attack of birds. Beside the gooseberry wire grew a row of rhubarb. Each clump was covered with the end of an old tub or pot drain-pipe with sacking over the top.

Extract 3

Skating

Hatty and Tom skated on and on. The skaters they met now were mostly men. There were few girls, that Tom could see, and none without escort. They came to a lonely river-side alehouse: its signboard said: 'The Five Miles from Anywhere—No Hurry'. Here there were skaters, labourers from the Fen farms, resting on the bank. They called out jovially to Hatty, asking if she would like any of them to skate with her for company. They went on calling, until she called back that she had a companion with her, even if they could not see him. The skaters thought this a good hoax and laughed, taking no offence; and Hatty laughed; and Tom laughed too, but no one except Hatty heard him.

They skated on, and the thin, brilliant sun was beginning to set, and Hatty's black shadow flitted along at their right hand, across the dazzle of the ice. Sometimes they skated on the main river; sometimes they skated along the flooded washes. Only the willows along the bank watched them; and the ice hissed with their passage.

They had stopped talking or thinking—their legs and arms and bodies seemed to throw from side to side with the precise, untiring regularity of clock-pendulums—long before Hatty cried: 'Look, Tom—the tower of Ely cathedral!'

From the river, however, Ely's tower plays a game with the traveller. Hatty and Tom skated and skated, and for a long time the tower seemed to let them come no nearer, but performed a mysterious movement instead, now to one side, now to the other, now ahead, according to the windings of the river. At last, however, they were certainly getting nearer, and now the cathedral tower began to disappear behind the nearer rooftops; and here they were where the river curves in to the town of Ely.

Extract 4

All you need to know about measles

Measles (or Rubeola) is a highly infectious and deadly disease. The measles virus is airborne, which means that it is passed on by coughs, sneezes, saliva and mucus. Until after 1954, when the first successful vaccine was developed, there was no effective way to prevent the disease from spreading.

Measles starts with flu-like symptoms. This occurs about four days before the person realises they have it. Three to five days later, a rash appears inside the mouth and spreads to the face and then all over the body. A patient is contagious four days before and after the rash appears. Once a person has measles, there is no cure. The only treatment is to rest, drink lots of liquid and stay away from others who have not had the disease or the vaccine. In serious cases, the patient can develop diarrhoea, blindness, bronchitis leading to pneumonia and inflammation of the brain that causes severe headaches. Measles is very harmful and often fatal in pregnancy.

In the past, measles spread quickly. An outbreak of measles could wipe out whole communities, particularly in areas of poor hygiene and quarantine. People had to be extremely careful to avoid contact with someone with measles. Children under the age of five were most at risk and millions of children died from the disease worldwide.

Today, measles is uncommon and almost forgotten. Vaccination programmes have almost eliminated the disease. However, some people opt not to use it for religious, philosophical or personal reasons. This has led to modern outbreaks of the disease and renewed efforts to educate and vaccinate.

GRAMMAR, PUNCTUATION & SPELLING ▶

1. Hyphen or dash?

Objective
To identify how dashes are used.

What you need
Copies of *Tom's Midnight Garden*.

What to do

- Briefly revise hyphens and dashes. (Dashes are longer than hyphens and serve a different purpose: dashes emphasise a part of the text, whereas hyphens link parts of a compound word – particularly to avoid ambiguity.) Demonstrate how meaning is clarified in this example: a *light-brown* basket as opposed to a *light, brown* basket.

- Write up the main uses for dashes on the board (setting off material in parenthesis, emphasising the sentence conclusion, breaking up dialogue to indicate a pause or omission). For each use, invite an example to demonstrate the function.

- The author uses dashes liberally in *Tom's Midnight Garden*. Re-read Chapter 1 together and at each example of a dash, invite a volunteer to give its purpose. Ask: *What other punctuation could have been used? What is the effect of using dashes?* (Depending on context: brackets, commas, colon or ellipsis; dashes are more dramatic and draw attention to a part of the text or break/pause.)

- Organise the children into small groups and allocate each a different chapter to scan for dashes and identify how they are used. Share their findings as a class at the end.

Differentiation

Support: Organise mixed ability groups and ensure that each child has a turn suggesting how the dashes are used.

Extension: Encourage the children to scan several chapters and then to compare how the author uses dashes here with other books they have read.

2. Letter strings

Objective
To spell words containing the letter string 'ough'.

What you need
Photocopiable page 22 'Letter strings', dictionaries.

What to do

- When Tom climbs the tree in Chapter 6, point out the word 'bough' and write it on the board. Ask the children to look it up in a dictionary, and invite a volunteer to say it and give its meaning. Ask: *What word sounds the same but has a different meaning and spelling?* (bow)

- Ask small groups to list words that sound like 'bough'. Then build a class list on the board, categorising their suggestions by spelling sound/letter string. ('now', 'cow', 'brow', 'allow', 'miaow'; 'plough', 'drought')

- Now ask groups to list words containing the 'ough' letter string. When inviting examples, focus on the different sounds 'ough' makes (for example 'tough', 'though', 'through', 'thought').

- Hand out photocopiable page 22 'Letter strings' for individuals to complete.

- Bring the class together at the end and invite volunteers to use the words in sentences, checking pronunciation.

Differentiation

Support: Allow them to practise by saying each word aloud before writing it down.

Extension: Ask groups to research other words with the same letter string and use them in sentences with correct pronunciation.

3. Separating clauses

Objective

To use colons and semicolons to separate independent clauses.

What you need

Copies of *Tom's Midnight Garden*.

What to do

- Briefly revise the core features of a sentence (subject, finite verb, capital to start and full stop to end, or equivalent). Explain that sometimes authors use colons or semicolons between independent clauses (sentences) in place of a full stop. (A semicolon shows two clauses are closely linked; it's often used to replace 'and' or 'but'. A colon may be used to connect two sentences where the second sentence summarises or explains the first.)

- Pearce frequently uses colons and semicolons to separate independent clauses. Point out that this may reflect a writing style more common in the mid-20th century and encourage them to compare it to their independent readers or other novels written in the same era.

- Organise groups. Ask them to choose a chapter to read together, noting pages with examples of semicolons or colons separating independent clauses. (Remind them that colons and semicolons do also have other functions – see the 'Listing' activity.)

- Hold a plenary session at the end, inviting groups to share examples for discussion with the rest of the class, giving page numbers.

Differentiation

Support: Guide them to good examples, such as Chapter 6 where Tom pushes through a door (colons) or Chapter 13 where Tom goes to bed with a cold (semicolons).

Extension: Ask them to choose a relevant passage to rewrite with full stops, rather than colons and semicolons, then discuss the different effect.

4. Listing

Objective

To investigate using colons and semicolons in lists.

What you need

Copies of *Tom's Midnight Garden*, example lists, descriptive clauses.

What to do

- Begin by asking: *What sort of lists do you come across regularly?* (shopping lists, 'to do' lists, class registers, kit lists, team lists) Provide examples to discuss, focusing on features and layout (for example, bullets, one item under another, alphabetical order, colons to introduce).

- Ask: *How do you usually separate list items in a paragraph?* (comma between each list item with 'and' separating the final two – discuss use of the serial comma) Ask: *Do you always need a colon to introduce a list?* (Not if it's part of a sentence; it flows on naturally.)

- Write on the board: 'gravelled, box-edged paths, dense, tangled hedges, delicate, pink, heavy-scented hyacinths'. Invite a volunteer to write them in a list in a sentence, following 'Tom saw…'. Discuss the comma overload and how semicolons can separate list items for clarity.

- Ask groups to scan Chapter 3 for lists, noting page numbers.

- Bring them together and discuss the lists' features. Ask: *Do they start with a colon?* (No, they are part of a sentence.) *Why do they have semicolons?* (List items contain commas, or are longer than one or two words.) Demonstrate how each list item is parallel in grammatical form. Scan other chapters for lists and discuss features together.

Differentiation

Support: Provide them with a bank of descriptive clauses to organise and write after a sentence starter.

Extension: Ask them to write a paragraph containing a descriptive list that requires semicolons.

5. In context

Objective

To increase awareness of homophones and other easily confused words.

What you need

Copies of *Tom's Midnight Garden*, photocopiable page 23 'In context', dictionaries.

What to do

- Discuss with the class how spelling is often determined by context to elicit their knowledge of homophones and other easily confused words. Ask: *What do you call words that sound alike but have different meanings and even spellings, such as 'too', 'two' and 'to'?* (homophones)

- Clarify the difference between homophones and homographs (same spelling, different sound and meaning). Write 'bow', 'wind' and 'wound' on the board and invite pairs to think of sentences to demonstrate the different meanings and pronunciations.

- Now, write these words on the board: 'bald', 'night', 'raw', 'prophet' and 'threw'. Invite the class to identify a homophone for each and write it next to its pair on the board. Then ask pairs of volunteers to use the homophones in sentences. Discuss ways of differentiating the spellings to help remember which one to use, such as mnemonics.

- Hand out photocopiable page 23 'In context' for them to complete independently.

- When they finish, encourage them to check their work with a partner and discuss any differences, confirming with use of a dictionary.

Differentiation

Support: Provide cards with homophones on for the children to match up in small groups.

Extension: Ask pairs to research homophones in a chapter of the novel and to make a poster demonstrating how to use their identified word and its homophone in context.

6. Will I or won't I?

Objective

To use modal verbs to indicate degrees of possibility.

What you need

Photocopiable page 24 'Will I or won't I?'

What to do

- Write some common modals on the board ('would', 'should', 'can', 'could', 'must', 'might', 'may', 'will'). Explain that they are special auxiliary verbs that don't usually work alone. Invite volunteers to use them in sentences to investigate how they work with other verbs in different tenses. Discuss what they do as a class (they show how possible something is, or how likely it is to happen or have happened – unlike 'be' and 'have' which help form tenses).

- Experiment together with degrees of possibility: 'might', 'may', 'must' and so on.

- Now invite volunteers to use the modals in their negative form. Start with an example on the board: 'Tom <u>can't</u> believe his uncle and aunt are lying.' Ask: *How can I turn this sentence into a question?* (Invert the subject and modal and add a question mark: '<u>Can't Tom</u> believe…<u>?</u>') Encourage examples and explore whether all questions using modals work this way – in negative or positive form.

- Discuss how modals can also indicate permission ('may', 'can'), ability ('can', 'could'), and obligation/ advice ('must', 'should').

- Hand out photocopiable page 24 'Will I or won't I?' for them to complete in pairs.

- When they finish, invite them to compare answers with another pair and discuss any differences.

Differentiation

Support: Allow them to omit the last activity on the photocopiable sheet.

Extension: Encourage them to use modals in sentences to express obligation, permission and ability.

Letter strings

- Write each word into the correct sound box below. Which words don't rhyme with the words in the sound boxes?

| ought | tough | fought | enough | cough | brought | though | dough | bought | nought |
| sought | plough | through | thorough | although | bough | drought | rough | borough | thought |

1. Words that rhyme with:

out	off	blue	sew	fluff	allow	sport

2. Words that don't rhyme:

- Now choose four of the words and use each of them in a sentence about Tom's Midnight Garden.

1. _____

2. _____

3. _____

4. _____

In context

● Match the words in the box below with their homophones in the table. Write each word in the correct column.

we'll	flower	pores	rain	write	way	guessed	pours
weal	paws	reign	wright	whey	eight	rite	toad

pause	wheel	guest	right	weigh	rein

● Write the three words from the table above which don't have a partner and add a suitable homophone next to each one.

1. _____   _____

2. _____   _____

3. _____   _____

● Choose the correct homophone to complete each of the sentences below.

1. Tom felt the chill of a _____ [*draft/draught*] on his back and he remembered that the door to the garden was open.

2. Tom counted the clock striking. Six! Seven! _____ [*ate/eight*]! Nine!

3. After opening the door, Tom was surprised to see a lawn, _____-beds [*flower/flour*] and trees.

4. Every _____ [*night/knight*] Tom sneaked downstairs into the garden.

5. The first tree Tom ever climbed was a _____ [*you/yew*]. Now he liked them the best.

Will I or won't I?

● Choose a suitable modal verb to complete each sentence. Use each modal only once.

> **would**   **won't**   **might**
>
> **can't**   **mustn't**

1. That _____ be right: the clock struck thirteen.

2. Aunt Gwen told Tom he _____ get out of bed.

3. Tom thought he _____ have been dreaming.

4. Hatty decided she _____ spy on Peter.

5. I _____ be lying if time after midnight doesn't count.

● Underline the modal verb and then turn each sentence into a question.

1. I can go outside into the garden.

_____

2. 'You would rather go home,' said Aunt Gwen.

_____

3. Tom should tell Peter all about the Midnight Garden.

_____

4. You couldn't have opened the door to the orchard.

_____

● Make up two sentences of your own about the book that contain modal verbs.

1. _____

_____

2. _____

_____

PLOT, CHARACTER & SETTING ▶

1. Tom

> **Objective**
>
> To consider how authors have developed characters and create a character profile.
>
> **What you need**
>
> Copies of *Tom's Midnight Garden*, photocopiable page 29 'Tom'.

What to do

- Re-read Chapter 1, with volunteers taking the speaking parts: Tom, mother, Uncle Alan, Aunt Gwen. Encourage them to focus on Tom: his age, family, what he's like – feelings, reactions and character. At the end, ask: *What do you already know about Tom?* (Focus on factual evidence: parents, brother; enjoys tree-climbing, hasn't had measles.) *How old is Tom?* (infer from interests, way his mother speaks to him)

- Ask: *Do you like Tom? Why?* Encourage reasons and gather adjectives describing him. Ask: *Do you think the author wants you to like him or feel sorry for him? Why?* (Focus on the words: 'anger', 'bitterly', 'angrily', 'rude', 'poky', 'disappointed', 'burst out', 'suspicions', 'condescendingly', and how Tom's thoughts are included.)

- Hand out photocopiable page 29 'Tom' and demonstrate how to analyse the text with questions. For example, ask: *How does Aunt Gwen try to make Tom feel welcome?* (flowers) *How does Tom react to his room? Why?* (He's upset, he sees bars as babyish.)

- Track Tom's character development from words and evidence in the text as you read or as a revision activity, reflecting on how he matures and changes. Regularly share ideas.

> **Differentiation**
>
> **Support:** Select limited chapters for children to analyse.
>
> **Extension:** Ask groups to compare how they might feel about how Tom reacts.

2. Making comparisons

> **Objectives**
>
> To make comparisons.
>
> **What you need**
>
> Copies of *Tom's Midnight Garden*.
>
> **Cross-curricular link**
>
> History

What to do

- Revise Chapter 1. Ask: *What sort of home do the Kitsons live in?* (a big house converted into flats) *Why do you think it was converted?* Discuss the historical context of large houses (servants, no modern facilities; houses became too expensive to be homes and so were sold or converted to flats, homes for the elderly, hospitals). Ask: *Have you ever been to a big house like this?* (For example, on a school trip.)

- Ask: *What are Tom's first impressions of the Kitsons' home?* (crowded by other houses; oblong, plain, grave) Now invite a volunteer to read as Tom steps inside their hall. Discuss his reaction, focusing on the links to the senses: sight, smell, feel. Ask: *What's the only sound?* (clock ticking)

- Ask them to read independently the description of the hall in the night in Chapter 6. Ask: *How are the hall, house and garden different after the clock strikes thirteen?* Encourage descriptive comparisons and guide them to contrast mood and visual aspects. Ask: *What objects from the hall can you imagine having or not having in your house?* Look for reasoned answers.

> **Differentiation**
>
> **Extension:** Invite pairs to discuss and compare the Kitsons' flat (Chapter 1) and the big house (Chapter 6) to their homes.

3. Out of control

Objective
To summarise the main ideas drawn from more than one paragraph.

What you need
Copies of *Tom's Midnight Garden*, poster board, dictionaries, access to the Internet.

Cross-curricular links
Art, science.

What to do

- Ask: *Why do people visit famous gardens?* Accept thoughtful answers, bearing in mind the children's different experiences of gardens in towns and the countryside. Ask whether anyone has visited a public garden. Invite volunteers to share memories and build a word- and phrase-bank to describe gardens (kitchen garden, greenhouse, lawns, summer house, sundial).

- Organise the children into groups to skim Chapters 3 and 5. Ask them to list everything Tom encounters in the garden. Encourage children to notice and appreciate the detail in the vivid descriptions. Provide dictionaries and also reference tools (the Internet and books) to find out what everything might look like, such as yew trees, hyacinths and humus.

- Give each group a poster board and explain that they will make a collage of the garden Tom discovers to send to Tom's brother, Peter. They can experiment with a simple birds-eye outline and then gradually build on it by adding line drawings like in the novel, or coloured pictures and images they have drawn or collected.

- Finally, each person in the group can choose descriptive or evocative words and phrases from the book to add to the collage.

Differentiation
Support: Allow them to build their collage from only the details given in Chapter 3.

Extension: Challenge them to design an advertisement encouraging people to visit the Midnight Garden.

4. Creating atmosphere

Objective
To identify and discuss themes and conventions, including atmosphere.

What you need
Copies of *Tom's Midnight Garden*, photocopiable page 30 'A change in atmosphere'.

What to do

- After finishing Chapter 6, hand out photocopiable page 30 'A change in atmosphere' and explain that they will use it to chart changes in the atmosphere, using textual evidence.

- Complete the first part together. Focus on how atmosphere is created, guiding them with questions. Ask: *What is the atmosphere when Tom begins to explore the garden?* (happy and joyous) *What words and techniques create this?* List their ideas on the board, backed by evidence in the text. (Point out links to the setting: weather/ season; rich descriptions of flowers and plants; sensory experiences; positive words and vivid colours; Tom doing what he loves.)

- Before they complete the chart independently, use questions to ascertain whether they notice where the atmosphere changes. Ask: *When does the atmosphere begin to change?* (When Tom's frustrated; he is unable to explore beyond the door and learns to push through.) *What signifies the change?* (mostly the wording expressing Tom's frustration: 'glares', 'slammed', 'barrier') *What makes him begin to feel uneasy?* (constant fine weather, unpredictable times of day and season, feeling of being watched) *How does the atmosphere towards the end contrast with the start?* (heavy and dark, contrasting with Tom's joy at the start)

Differentiation
Support: Provide page references, guiding them on where to focus.

Extension: Encourage them to write a diary entry as Tom, recording what he thinks has happened and how the fir tree has reappeared.

5. Discovering Hatty

> **Objective**
>
> To consider how authors have developed characters.
>
> **What you need**
>
> Copies of *Tom's Midnight Garden*, wallchart card, sticky notes.

What to do

- Ask the children to read Chapters 8 to 10 in groups. Encourage them to use sticky notes to record page references where the author provides information about Hatty and what they found out. Encourage them to categorise their findings into facts about Hatty (green pencil) and things that tell them about her personality and character (blue pencil).

- Bring the class together to share their findings. Place their sticky notes onto a wallchart, clustering similar findings.

- Now ask: *How did you find out this information about Hatty?* (via the narrator/author or inferred from what Hatty says and does) Explain that although the story has a third-person narrator, the reader still only knows what Tom knows about Hatty. Then list together what the children don't know about Hatty (for example, they know nothing about her background).

- As you progress through the book, encourage the children to keep using sticky notes to piece together Hatty's background for the wallchart, focusing on *how* they find out.

- Examine the author's techniques that allow Tom and the reader to find out (the aunt speaking to Hatty after the geese incident; seeing Hatty as a younger, weeping child; James' conversation with his mother; finally what Mrs Bartholomew tells Tom at the end).

> **Differentiation**
>
> **Extension:** Ask them to write a paragraph to explain why Hatty pretended she was a princess. Encourage prediction and empathy based on their knowledge of her.

6. Questions, questions

> **Objective**
>
> To ask questions to improve their understanding.
>
> **What you need**
>
> Copies of *Tom's Midnight Garden*.

What to do

- This activity can be used at any point in the novel.

- Begin by asking: *Why do we ask questions?* (It helps check recall and understanding.) Write these questions on the board: *What day is it today? What is your favourite subject and why? What is the value of learning science?* Then, ask: *Which question would be easiest to answer? Why?* (The first is easier as it is factual, requiring simple recall; the second and third require reflection and thought.)

- Hold a class discussion on the different question types, inviting volunteers to invent questions and decide in which category they belong.

- Write up these questions on the latest chapter and ask them to jot down answers. Ask: *What happened in this chapter? Why is this chapter important in the plot?* Survey which question they found quicker or easier to answer and why.

- Organise them into pairs to invent questions for another pair (three closed/factual questions and three open or thinking/reflective questions on the chapter or book so far).

- After a set time, invite pairs to hold Q&A sessions with another pair and then another.

> **Differentiation**
>
> **Support:** Pair children strategically and allow them to write two factual questions and one open question for their Q&A.
>
> ---
>
> **Extension:** Ask them to prepare a set of written comprehension questions for a partner, including a range of question types. Answers can be written down and marked by each other.

7. Time passing

Objective
To identify how structure contributes to meaning, focusing on the passing of time.

What you need
Copies of *Tom's Midnight Garden*, photocopiable page 31 'Timelines'.

What to do

- Begin with a discussion about memories. Ask: *What's your earliest/favourite/funniest memory?* Share memories of your own and ask: *What do you want to do in your future?* If appropriate, share what you wanted to do as a child and compare it to what you do now. Then read the paragraph in Chapter 18 beginning: 'Tom was thinking about the Past…'. Invite a volunteer to explain what it means in relation to the book's plot.

- Ask: *Is the plot narrated in chronological order?* (yes, in Tom's time; not in Hatty's – so no overall) *When did the story begin?* (Accept thoughtful answers, encouraging supportive examples.)

- Now organise the children into small groups to discuss the question: *Is the plot one story or two?* Invite a spokesperson from each group to share their answers and reasons.

- Hand out photocopiable page 31 'Timelines' for them to complete in pairs.

- When they have completed the timelines, pairs should choose one of the timelines each and write a paragraph summarising their timeline, using linking words to express the passing of time (such as 'first', 'then', 'next', 'while', 'after which').

Differentiation
Support: Provide pairs with a framework of linking words for their paragraph and allow them to fill in the events.

Extension: Ask pairs to combine their paragraphs into an overall summary of the plot's chronology, accompanied by a composite timeline.

8. Endings

Objective
To identify how structure, particularly endings, contribute to meaning.

What you need
Copies of *Tom's Midnight Garden*.

What to do

- After reading, invite a volunteer to summarise Chapter 25. Ask: *Why did Tom react to Aunt Gwen 'as if against a hateful sight'?* (He didn't want to wake up in his time.) *Why was Tom so upset when he couldn't get into the garden?* (It was his last chance to enter the garden; he hoped to see young Hatty again.)

- Remind them of the classic story structure and ask: *At what point in the story does this chapter fall?* (At the climax – encourage reasoned answers.)

- Organise the class into groups to predict what will happen next – how the story resolves. Encourage them to think back over the book for clues. Write key words on the board to guide them ('Hatty', 'skates', 'Mrs Bartholomew', 'clock', 'young Barty'). They should make notes for a spokesperson to share in a plenary.

- Read to the end of the book together and discuss the ending, both using and encouraging questions to boost reflection. (For example, ask: *What was different to your predictions? How satisfied are you? Are there any loose ends?*)

- Now ask them to write a paragraph explaining why they enjoyed/did not enjoy the ending, using linking words (such as, 'firstly', 'then', 'because', 'which meant', 'although', 'for example').

Differentiation
Support: Provide a paragraph frame for the children to complete: 'I enjoyed/did not enjoy the ending because…'; 'My favourite part was…'.

Extension: Challenge children to write a second paragraph comparing their predictions to the ending.

Tom

- Build up a profile of Tom from descriptive words or phrases and other evidence (actions, thoughts and illustrations).

Tom's appearance:	Page numbers:
Words:	
Evidence:	

What I think Tom is like:

Chapter:	Reasons:

How Tom has changed:

Chapter:	Reasons:

A change in atmosphere

- Use evidence from Chapter 6 to help you complete the table below. Include words, phrases, weather/season, sensory experiences and Tom's mood/thoughts.

Exploring the garden	Getting frustrated and uneasy	The storm
The atmosphere is:	The atmosphere is:	The atmosphere is:
Evidence:	Evidence:	Evidence:
Tom's mood/reactions:	Tom's mood/reactions:	Tom's mood/reactions:

- List adjectives below to describe the atmosphere created by the final paragraph.

Timelines

● Complete these timelines by adding events to each one in chronological order. Add more lines if you need to.

Tom's time

Year: _____

Season: _____

Hatty's time

Historical period: _____

Approximate date: _____

Try to include the season with each event you list on the timeline below.

TALK ABOUT IT ▶

1. Interview the characters

Objectives

To consider different viewpoints and participate in role play.

What you need

Copies of *Tom's Midnight Garden*, photocopiable page 35 'Interview the characters'.

What to do

- Read Chapter 1 together and ask the children to name the characters mentioned (Tom, Tom's mother, Peter, Uncle Alan, Aunt Gwen, Mrs Bartholomew).

- Have a class discussion about how each person is feeling and why. Find clues in the chapter and consider the way they speak and what they say.

- Organise the children into groups of seven to include the characters and an interviewer. Children can choose which characters they want to be.

- Working together, ask them to invent questions they think are relevant to each character and write them on photocopiable page 35 'Interview the characters'. Remind the children to use open-ended questions, not closed ones. For example: to Tom's mother – *Why must Tom leave? Is this the best solution?*; to Tom – *Why do you feel so angry about leaving?*; to Peter – *What are you going to do without Tom?*; to Uncle Alan – *How do you feel about Tom's visit?*; to Aunt Gwen – *What plans and arrangements have you made for Tom?*; to Mrs Bartholomew – *Are there any rules you'd like Tom to know about?*

- Provide time for groups to practise answering the questions using clues from the text and their own interpretation of the situation, before presenting to the class with clarity and confidence.

Differentiation

Extension: Use other scenarios to interview the characters, such as when Hatty has a fall.

2. Stepping out

Objective

To gain, maintain and monitor the interest of the listener(s).

What you need

Copies of *Tom's Midnight Garden*, photocopiable page 36 'Stepping out'.

What to do

- Read the last sentence of Chapter 4 and then begin a class discussion about the author's concept of opening a door and stepping into a different world. Ask: *Do you like the idea? Does it make for a good story plot? Do you know any other books that use this technique? Can you think of any other ways to enter a different world?* Encourage ideas or knowledge of other novels, such as *The Lion, the Witch and the Wardrobe* and Pullman's *His Dark Materials*.

- Demonstrate by involving the class. Begin with something like: 'When the old school bell rang, I carefully but excitedly opened the classroom door.' Then ask one child to add on a sentence and then the next person has a turn and so on. Continue until everyone has added a sentence to the adventure.

- Now tell the children to work on their own. Hand out photocopiable page 36 'Stepping out' and ask the children to imagine themselves as the main character in a different story. They should design their new, imaginary world. Let them brainstorm ideas to use to guide their speaking.

- In groups, invite them to take turns to relate their scenario. The group should then have an opportunity to ask questions and give suggestions. Afterwards each group can select their favourite scenario to share with the class.

Differentiation

Extension: Encourage the children to write out their story in paragraphs.

3. Discuss a topic

Objective
To participate in discussions and debates.

What you need
Copies of *Tom's Midnight Garden*, Extract 4.

Cross-curricular link
PSHE

What to do

- Various themes in the novel highlight topics and issues that are still relevant to children today. Refer to Extract 4 and invite them to identify the issue (measles). Ask: *How does this feature in the novel?* Next, scan the chapters for other issues. (Chapter 2: bedtime rules and authority; Chapters 3 and 4: white lies or things adults tell children to make them behave; Chapters 8 and 9: bullying; Chapter 15: graffiti.)

- Display these questions: *What is your experience of this issue? What is your opinion on it? What do you think is the correct way to handle it? Is anyone responsible or to blame?*

- Each issue has different perspectives. Ask the children to choose one issue and create two columns to record differing thoughts. On one side, invite them to note how they feel about the issue using the questions to guide their thoughts. Then, in groups, encourage discussion of others' views and write these different views on the other side.

- After groups have had time to discuss the issues, invite volunteers to report back to the class.

Differentiation

Support: Work through one issue together, such as bullying. Find examples in the text where Hatty is bullied and talk about their own experiences and possible solutions.

Extension: Conduct a debate on one of the topics that interests them, for example: 'It's your right to choose not to vaccinate against measles'.

4. Act it out

Objective
To participate in role play, speaking audibly and fluently.

What you need
Copies of *Tom's Midnight Garden*.

What to do

- Invite volunteers to read the following scenes aloud: Chapter 9 where Hatty sticks out her tongue at Tom (four characters); the end of Chapter 9 and beginning of Chapter 10 where Tom and Hatty introduce themselves (two characters); the argument in Chapter 13 between Tom and Hatty (two characters); Chapter 21, where Tom and Uncle Alan talk (three characters).

- Arrange the children in groups according to which scene they are going to role play. In their groups, tell them to read the relevant part of the text a few times, taking turns to read their speaking parts.

- Encourage the groups to adapt the extract to perform in front of the class without a narrator. They should use the dialogue in the book, but add to it or change it so that it flows well.

- Discuss some stage rules and write them on the board (face the audience when you speak; know your position; speak audibly and fluently; use confident body language).

- If time permits, allow the children to dress up and use basic props.

- When the children perform their role play, encourage the audience to focus by using the list on the board to note the things they see in action.

Differentiation

Extension: Challenge them to invent a scene/dialogue from the novel to act out, like a private conversation between Uncle Alan and Aunt Gwen, or a dialogue between Hatty and her cousins.

5. Build your vocabulary

Objective

To use relevant strategies to build their vocabulary.

What you need

Copies of *Tom's Midnight Garden*, poster paper, marker pens, dictionaries.

Cross-curricular link

History

What to do

- Read together Chapter 17, where Tom enters the Melbournes' house. Ask the children what they notice about the vocabulary and language in the story (not a modern way of speaking – some unfamiliar vocabulary). Then read the extract again; this time ask them to identify specific, unfamiliar words like 'capes', 'pumps', 'gaiters', 'waders', 'spats', 'inkwell', 'round ruler of ebony', 'washstand', 'basin' and 'ewer'. Discuss the meaning of these words and try to categorise them (clothes, stationery, household equipment).

- Write the following title on the board: 'Building vocabulary'. Then write any of the following categories underneath: fashion; transport; games/activities; homes and gardens; equipment; health and food; expressions.

- Divide the class into small groups. Give each group a large piece of poster paper and divide it into four. Give each group four topics and ask them to skim the whole novel to find words and phrases that fit each topic. Once they have the words, provide dictionaries for them to find their meanings and write them on the poster paper beside each word.

- Provide each group with an opportunity to present its vocabulary list to the class.

- Display the vocabulary posters around the class.

Differentiation

Support: Limit the categories for each group according to ability, time and pace.

Extension: Invite the children to make up their own sentences using the words.

6. The way things were

Objective

To participate in presentations, speaking audibly and fluently.

What you need

Copies of *Tom's Midnight Garden*, photocopiable page 37 'The way things were'.

Cross-curricular link

History

What to do

- Ask the children to identify the eras of the main characters in the story. (Hatty is from the late Victorian era, Tom is from the mid-20th century.)

- Invite a class discussion about the way things were 'in those days', using examples from the story. Talk about how things have changed, for example Aunt Gwen sends a telegram to Tom's mother but today we send messages from a mobile phone or other device.

- Explain that they will prepare a speech on some aspect of life from one of the two eras. As a class, discuss ideas for interesting topics relating to the story, such as: modes of communication (letters, mail coaches, telegrams); fashion and clothing; servants; time devices (like grandfather clocks and pocket watches).

- The children can work individually or in pairs to research and prepare a presentation. Use photocopiable page 37 'The way things were' to guide their planning.

- Give each child an opportunity to present to the class.

Differentiation

Support: Allow the children's speech to be more general about the difference between 'then' and 'now', mainly using information gathered from the novel.

Extension: Bring in 'old' objects to display. Challenge them to discuss and then label each object.

Interview the characters

● Think of questions to ask the characters to find out how they felt and why they behaved as they did in the scene you have been discussing. Remember to ask open-ended questions.

Chapter and scene: _____

Character's name: _____

1. _____
2. _____
3. _____

Character's name: _____

1. _____
2. _____
3. _____

Character's name: _____

1. _____
2. _____
3. _____

Character's name: _____

1. _____
2. _____
3. _____

Stepping out

- Imagine stepping into a new world. Plan your experience here.

Title: _____

Main character:

Other characters:

Sketch this scene:

Era/time:

Past ☐

Present ☐

Future ☐

How you enter this world:

Describe what you see and do in this imaginary world.

The way things were

• Use this page to help you prepare and present.

Topic: _____

Intro (clear and catchy)
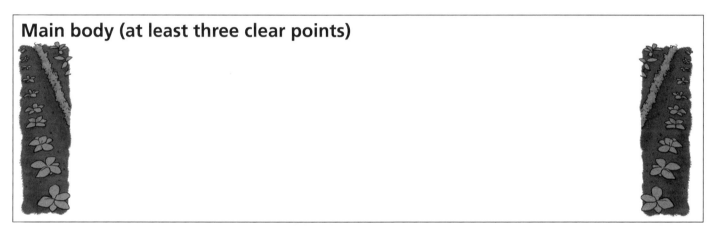

Main body (at least three clear points)

Conclusion (clear and concise)

Checklist	Not yet	Yes
1. Have you practised your presentation? Are you familiar with what you will be saying?	☐	☐
2. Can your audience hear you? Are you using clear and natural speech?	☐	☐
3. Are you using confident body language?	☐	☐

GET WRITING ▶

1. Making headlines

> **Objectives**
>
> To recognise vocabulary and structures that are appropriate for formal speech.
>
> **What you need**
>
> Copies of *Tom's Midnight Garden*, news articles, marker pens, photocopiable page 41 'Making headlines'.

What to do

- In groups, let the children read some news articles. Using different coloured markers, ask them to highlight the headline and then the answers to these questions, noting the paragraph the answers were found in: *What happened? Who was involved? Where did it happen? When did this happen? How and why did it happen?* With another colour, highlight any direct speech.

- Come together and ask: *What do you expect to find in a news article?* (current, relevant news) *What is the writing style?* (formal and factual) *What is the purpose of a headline?* (to catch the reader's attention and summarise a topic) *Why is the main information in the first paragraph?* (to provide the most important facts first) *Does the direct speech reflect a dialogue or quotations?* (usually a quote) *What is the difference between facts and opinions?*

- Read together Chapter 12, where the geese destroy the garden. Ask them to imagine being a reporter on the scene. Ask: *Who would you interview? What questions would you ask? What information would you gather?* Discuss answers.

- Hand out photocopiable page 41 'Making headlines' for them to plan their report on the geese incident. Provide time for them to write, edit and present a news report, working independently or in pairs.

> **Differentiation**
>
> **Support:** Encourage them to role play and write an interview with the family. Together, differentiate between facts and opinions.

2. Step-by-step

> **Objectives**
>
> To use organisational and presentational devices to structure text.
>
> **What you need**
>
> Copies of *Tom's Midnight Garden*.

What to do

- While Tom and Hatty were building a tree house, Peter began to build one too. Ask: *Has anyone built a tree house? How did you do it? What would you need? What precautions should you take?* Listen to and discuss their comments.

- Work together to write instructions on the board for how to build a tree house. Model the layout for instructions, with headings including: topic, things you need, steps, precautions. Divide the instructions into simple steps. Use numbers or sentence starters such as 'first', 'then', 'finally'.

- Reflect on what you've done. Ask: *Are the instructions in the correct order? Are all items listed? Is the wording clear and easy to follow?* Demonstrate how to start each instruction in the same way, for example with a command verb.

- Discuss other 'How to' ideas that relate to the novel. For example, how to: move through a door (Chapter 6); play hide-and-seek (Chapter 8); make a bow and arrow (Chapter 11); clean old skates (Chapter 22). Ask them to plan and write their own instructions. If time permits, they can draw and label a diagram to go with their set of instructions.

> **Differentiation**
>
> **Support:** Allow children to make up ten rules for: the garden, the house, bedtime, meal times, a game.
>
> ---
>
> **Extension:** Encourage them to produce instructions that require further research, such as how to wind a grandfather clock, how to send a telegram or how to play chess.

3. A new chapter

Objective
To describe settings, characters and atmosphere and integrate dialogue.

What you need
Copies of *Tom's Midnight Garden*, photocopiable page 42 'A new chapter'.

What to do

- In pairs, ask the children to skim through the chapters and note the garden scenes Tom finds each time he enters the garden. Ask: *What's the same? What has changed? What does he notice about Hatty and the cousins?* (They're older/ younger each time and their activities change accordingly.)

- The author was inspired by her own experience of growing up and playing with her siblings in a beautiful garden, where her own father had also been raised. Her happy childhood memories influenced the activities that her characters got up to. Ask the children to imagine another chapter the author could have included in the story. Discuss some new chapter titles and write ideas on the board.

- Invite the children to plan a new chapter for the book. Ask them to give their chapter a title and then write a detailed scene with dialogue between the characters (Hatty, Tom, Abel and the cousins). Tell them to use photocopiable page 42 'A new chapter' to plan their ideas. They should write a draft and then present an edited version to read to the class.

Differentiation
Support: Allow the children to choose an existing scene from the book and add new dialogue.

Extension: Challenge them to write a whole new chapter.

4. Design a survey

Objective
To use organisational and presentational devices to structure text.

What you need
Photocopiable page 43 'Games survey'.

Cross-curricular links
Maths, PSHE

What to do

- Tom and Hatty loved playing games in the garden. Ask: *What games did they play?*

- Write the following topic on the board: 'Favourite games'. Then list the following under the heading: 'Electronic/video games'; 'games in the park/ playground'; 'board games'; 'sports matches'; 'card games'; 'hoaxes'.

- Conduct a general class survey. Ask: *What's your favourite type of game?* Next to each type of game, write the names of the children to indicate their number one choice. Discuss the results by asking: *Which games seem to be most/least popular? Why?* Invite the children to consider other questions that they could ask to get information such as: *How often do you play your favourite game?*

- Hand out photocopiable page 43 'Games survey' and go through the questions, options and layout. The children should fill it in individually, then sit in groups and compare their answers. Using the results, ask them to write a short summary paragraph and report back to the class.

- In pairs, tell them to design their own survey. Consider topics such as bullying, sleep habits or food. Can the children invent questions for the survey and consider ways to present each question?

Differentiation
Support: Allow them to base their new survey on the one provided.

Extension: Ask them to indicate the results of a question using a pie chart or bar graph.

5. Mrs Bartholomew

Objective

To ensure the consistent use of tense and subject–verb agreement throughout a piece of writing.

What you need

Copies of *Tom's Midnight Garden*, biography of Philippa Pearce ('About the author', page 8).

What to do

- In groups, ask the children to recall everything they know about Mrs Bartholomew. Let them compile a timeline of events in her life, estimating her age. The start of the timeline is vague, so suggest they begin with 'born and raised in England by both parents'. The next known event would be her parents' death and moving to live with her aunt. Provide time for them to create the timeline. Come together, share ideas and discuss different views.

- Read aloud the short biography of Philippa Pearce. Ask them to identify the textual features and write them on the board (title, dates, chronological order, past tense, mostly factual, a type of summary).

- Using the timeline, ask them to work on their own to write a biography about Mrs Bartholomew, using the past tense. They should aim to include at least three paragraphs, one for each phase of her life (before the garden, in the garden, after the garden).

- Remind them to write their first draft, share it with a partner, edit and then write a final version.

Differentiation

Support: Revise past tense together. Write the main events on the board and ask them to order them.

Extension: Ask them to rewrite their biography as an autobiography using the first person and to add Mrs Bartholomew's personal reflections.

6. Contrasting images

Objective

To evaluate and edit by assessing the effectiveness of their own and others' writing.

What you need

Copies of *Tom's Midnight Garden*, paper or notebooks.

What to do

- Ask the children to think about contrasting images, events or scenes in the novel (the garden before and after the geese destroyed it; the garden in summer and then in winter; the hall by day and night; outside the back door by day and night; Hatty in her dress before and after she fell).

- Let them work with a partner and choose a contrasting image. Ask them to rule a line down the middle of a page in their notebooks. On one side, they should note the 'before' scene and on the other side the contrasting scene. Encourage them to use concise, but effective, language to describe each image in detail – before and after.

- With their partners, invite them to write two descriptive paragraphs – one before and one after. Encourage them to be original and develop their notes, using figurative language where appropriate. They should stick to the same tense for each to give a sense of continuity.

- Once partners have completed their paragraphs, encourage them to read their paragraphs aloud to the class. Ask the class to listen attentively and provide constructive feedback.

Differentiation

Support: Use a few images, but ask them to write one sentence to describe each image.

Extension: Invite them to write a contrasting poem of two stanzas – before and after. The poem should be free verse.

Making headlines

- Use this newspaper template to plan a news report.

Headline: _____

First paragraph (Who? What? Where? When? How? Why?):

_____
_____
_____
_____
_____
_____
_____
_____

Picture:

Caption:

Second paragraph (details and eyewitness accounts):

_____
_____
_____
_____
_____
_____
_____
_____

Final paragraph (conclusion):

_____
_____
_____
_____
_____
_____

Spot check

Spelling ☐
Punctuation ☐
Formal language ☐
Ordered information ☐

A new chapter

● Plan a new chapter in the story.

1. New chapter title: _____

2. Characters involved: _____

3. Chapter outline:

Scene 1	Scene 2
Scene 3	**Scene 4**

● Now write one scene of the chapter in detail with dialogue.

_____

_____

_____

_____

_____

_____

_____

_____

Games survey

- Complete this survey by ticking one box to answer each question.
- Sit in groups to compare and compile answers.

Survey topic: Favourite games

1. Choose or add your favourite type of game in the list below.

Electronic/video games ☐   Board games ☐

Ball games ☐   Card games ☐

Water games ☐   _____ games ☐

2. On average, how many hours per week do you play your favourite game?

0–1 hour ☐

2–4 hours ☐

5–6 hours ☐

7–9 hours ☐

10+ hours ☐

3. With whom do you prefer to play?

Alone ☐

With a partner ☐

With a small group ☐

With a big group ☐

With family ☐

4. Have you ever stayed up past your bedtime to play?

Yes ☐

No ☐

5. Have you ever cheated or given an incorrect score? (This question is not compulsory.)

Yes ☐

No ☐

Maybe ☐

ASSESSMENT ▶

1. Pay attention

Objective
To listen and respond appropriately.

What you need
Copies of *Tom's Midnight Garden.*

What to do

- Ask the children to sit comfortably and to listen to an extract. Turn to Chapter 15 where Tom decides to walk along the wall. Read from '"I'm going to walk along that wall."' to '"Tell me what you see," Hatty pleaded.'

- The author uses lots of descriptive detail which gives the reader a sense of being present. Ask: *How does Tom feel?* (Amazed, scared, triumphant.) *How does Hatty feel?* (Excited, nervous, jealous.)

- Ask them to name some of the things Tom could see from the wall and write them on the board. Then read the extract again and identify any missing items and add them to the list.

- Choose another extract, or go to Chapter 3 and read from 'Tom opened the door wide and let in the moonlight' to 'She was carrying paper, kindling wood and a box of matches.'

- After the reading, let them work in pairs to prepare a report back as if Tom were telling his aunt and uncle what he saw. The report back can be divided into two parts – what he saw in the garden and what he saw in the house. Use the first person 'I saw'. Give each pair a chance to report back.

Differentiation
Support: Allow pairs to focus their reports on either the garden or the house.

Extension: Ask them to write a letter from Tom to Peter describing what he saw, adding his personal comments.

2. Comprehend this

Objective
To understand what they read by asking and answering questions.

What you need
Copies of *Tom's Midnight Garden*, Extract 1, Extract 2, Extract 3, photocopiable page 47 'Comprehend this'.

What to do

- Explain to the children that they will be completing a reading task to check their understanding of a text. Use copies of any of the extracts as an example to show the different types of question.

- Revise and explain different types and levels of questions. Explain: closed (simple 'yes' or 'no' responses); open (require details); multiple choice (choose an answer from options); basic level (find the answer in the text); middle level (analyse information or classify); higher level (interpret and apply the information).

- Remind the children to skim the text for the context, read the questions before re-reading the text in detail, and finally attempt to write answers. Once they have followed these steps, they will be ready to begin. Write the steps on the board.

- Turn to Chapter 4 and explain that they should start where Tom decides to check if the garden is real ('As he ran down the stairs to the hall, Tom was remembering the hyacinths…') and finish at the end of the chapter.

- Hand out photocopiable page 47 'Comprehend this' and ask them to follow the steps to answer the questions independently.

Differentiation
Extension: Choose another extract and let them prepare different types of questions to ask each other.

3. Figure it out

Objective

To evaluate how authors use figurative language, considering the impact on the reader.

What you need

Copies of *Tom's Midnight Garden*, Extract 1, Extract 2, Extract 3, Extract 4.

What to do

- Check the children's understanding of literal and figurative language. Ask: *What's the difference between literal and figurative language*? (Literal language says things as they are; figurative language uses comparisons, expressions, images and wordplay to describe something.) Discuss types of figurative language that use comparisons. (Personification is when something is given human qualities; similes compare using 'like' or 'as'; metaphors compare without using the words 'like' or 'as'.)

- Work together and use all four extracts to show these examples: Extract 1 – 'imprisoned in wakefulness' (metaphor), 'the house seemed to hold its breath' (personification); Extract 2 – the sundial's 'chin was buried in curly stone clouds' (personification), 'like a child's arms' (simile); Extract 3 – 'the ice hissed with their passage' (personification); Extract 4 is an example of literal or factual language. Compare Extract 4 to the others and discuss the difference (mostly facts, no figurative language)

- Working in pairs, ask them to skim a chapter of their choice to find other examples of personification, similes and metaphors. Discuss their findings.

- Ask them to individually use another example from the story, identify the figurative language and provide an alternative example of figurative language to fit the context.

Differentiation

Support: Provide examples from the text or allocate a specific extract for use.

Extension: Encourage the children to review several other chapters for examples of personification, similes and metaphors.

4. Read aloud

Objective

To read aloud with accuracy and appropriate intonation to make the meaning clear.

What you need

Copies of *Tom's Midnight Garden*.

What to do

- Ask: *How would you describe the writing style in Tom's Midnight Garden? Is it easy or challenging to read? Why?* (Philippa Pearce wrote in a style used in the past. Hatty speaks the way people spoke in the Victorian era. When we read it, the style is unfamiliar and often unexpected.)

- To demonstrate this, ask the class to have copies of the book ready. Give them a page reference then choose someone to read aloud. Try to give everyone a chance to do some unprepared reading. Afterwards, discuss how they felt about it: whether they found it difficult or easy and why.

- Let them work in pairs to practise a prepared reading of a favourite extract from the story. Write the following on the board for them to focus on: 'accuracy', 'fluency', 'pronunciation', 'clarity' and 'expression'. Explain and discuss each term so the children understand what will be assessed.

- Give them time to practise their fluency with a partner and help each other to improve with feedback and suggestions.

- Give everyone a chance to read their extract aloud. Use the checklist to assess how well they did. Allow them to peer assess as well.

Differentiation

Support: The length of the text and level of difficulty should differ according to their ability.

Extension: Challenge them to read aloud to a different audience.

5. Respectfully yours

Objective

To recognise the difference between structures typical of informal and formal speech.

What you need

Copies of *Tom's Midnight Garden*.

Cross-curricular link

PSHE

What to do

- Ask: *How does Tom communicate with his brother, Peter?* (He writes letters.) *How would Tom write to Peter today?* (probably by text or email) Discuss how things have changed. Ask: *What letters are people most likely to write these days?* (formal ones – to lawyers or editors; thank you letters or letters of complaint)

- Ask: *How do you decide if a letter is formal or informal?* (Discuss the difference in purpose, style and tone.) *Did Tom write formal or friendly letters to Peter and how do you know?* (He wrote friendly letters, using informal speech, his own secret words like 'B.A.R.' and a special graphic signature.)

- Invite them to imagine Tom is writing a letter to Mrs Bartholomew to apologise (or to his aunt and uncle to thank them for his stay). Provide a framework on the board as a guide, showing them the correct structure and layout of a formal letter. Show them how to start and end the letter, reminding them to use three paragraphs (introduction, body and conclusion).

- Provide time for them to draft, edit and write or type out their final piece.

Differentiation

Support: Allow them to write a thank you letter to someone who has helped them out.

Extension: Ask them to write an email from Tom to Peter (or vice versa).

6. For sale

Objective

To give well-structured descriptions for different purposes, including for expressing feelings.

What you need

Copies of *Tom's Midnight Garden*, advertisements for houses in magazines and newspapers.

What to do

- Divide the board into two columns with the headings: 'Hatty's house then' and 'Hatty's house now'. In small groups, ask the children to highlight descriptions of the house as it was in the time of the Melbournes and how it is when the Kitsons live there (a set of flats). They can refer to the book to remind them.

- Provide magazines and examples of advertisements. Ask them to take turns to read aloud advertisements and then create a checklist of common selling techniques used in the advertisements. Write them on the board (clear purpose, positive language, figurative language, facts, appeals to the reader's/listener's desires, leading questions, ability to make negatives into positives, emotive language).

- Ask them to consider how they might use these selling techniques to sell the house in the novel – either as it was or as it is when the Kitsons live there. Discuss ideas and share examples.

- Arrange them into pairs. Explain that they must each take on the role of a salesperson, but from different times in the story. The first salesperson must prepare to sell Hatty's house as it was, the other salesperson must prepare to sell Hatty's house as it is.

- Allow time for them to plan, prepare and practise. Remind them to use the techniques on the board. Invite them to present their advertisements to the class.

Differentiation

Extension: Challenge them to write an advertisement for a newspaper or magazine based on their sales pitch.

Comprehend this

- Read Chapter 4 and then answer the questions below to show your understanding of the text.

1. What did Tom remember about the garden from last night?

_____

2. How was the lock on the back door different during the day and why did it make Tom feel ill?

_____

_____

_____

3. Explain what 'ginger beard' means when Tom is asked, "What's bitten you now?"

_____

_____

4. What do the initials B.A.R. stand for? Why did Tom use them in his letter to Peter?

B. _____ **A.** _____ **R.** _____

_____

5. Explain the meaning of 'prudence'.

_____

_____

6. Read the paragraph that includes 'Now he knew – he knew!'. Explain what Tom knew and how he knew it.

_____

_____

_____

7. What was Mrs Bartholomew doing when Tom entered the garden? Why do you think this detail is included?

_____

_____

Available in this series:

978-1407-16055-9

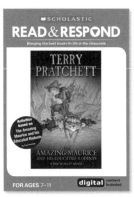

978-1407-16056-6

978-1407-16057-3

978-1407-16058-0

978-1407-16059-7

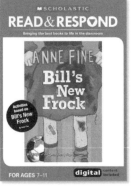

978-1407-16060-3

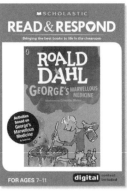

978-1407-16061-0

978-1407-16062-7

978-1407-16063-4

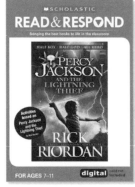

978-1407-16064-1

978-1407-16065-8

978-1407-16052-8

978-1407-16067-2

978-1407-16068-9

978-1407-16069-6

978-1407-16070-2

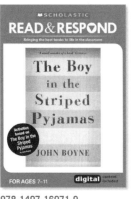

978-1407-16071-9

978-1407-17616-1

978-1407-17614-7

978-1407-17615-4

To find out more, call: 0845 6039091
or visit our website www.scholastic.co.uk/readandrespond